Playbook
for Muse-ical
Meditation & Mantra

A LI'TTLE
BOOK OF
CHANTS
FOR BIG
SOULS

BY YVETTE OM & JULIE FISCHER

This Playbook
is dedicated to
all those whose love for
self-knowledge and
creative song equals
an unparalleled calling
into the sacred.

Self knowledge + Song = Sacred

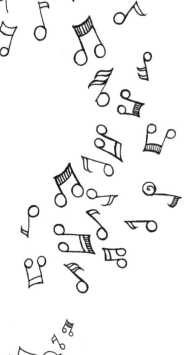

Illustrated by Joanne Fink

We have been blessed by the incredible artwork of Joanne Fink, as well as the additional beautiful contributions by Christopher Pecoraro and others.

Supplemental Illustrations:

Christopher Pecoraro
Pages 32, wheel
Page 6, 55-58: Feet
Pages 7-12: Elephant & Soul
Page 52: Flags
Pages 60-65: Hanuman
Pages 98, 100: Krishna

Samantha Trattner
Pages 114-117: Mandala

VectorStock
Pg 40: Avocado

Public domain
Pages 121, 121: Sri Yantra

Forward

From a tiny seed, an idea that my co-creator Julie Fischer had to compile this unique 'playbook' of chants, to this 124 pages of self exploration & creativity... my life once again affirms the mystery and magic inherent when we nurture something new and unknown through to its full manifestation. Isn't this what birthing is all about? While in morning meditation I ask myself again..." Who is actually birthing here?"

Sitting in a boxed room with open window or lounging on a white sanded beach while on tour in Florida, Julie and I would listen to one of my chants for a few moments and then from this meditative space I would speak about it. We recorded these words and Julie began framing them into a journal type format.

As all seeds are designed to germinate, we were blessed to connect with *Zenspirations* Joanne Fink, a dynamo spiritual seeker and artist who I had previously known in high school. Though Joanne was a year ahead of me, we were passing fellow school mates. In passing no more, a sweet friendship now is born.

Joanne took us under her generous and capable wings and our book map began to fill with these breathtaking and deeply reflective images.

And so from ethereal sound, mantra and voice we merge the spiritual journey with journaling, coloring, imaging and play.

How so? Each chapter includes an audio download from one of my 5 albums: *Into the Arms of Love, The Song of Breath, We Are One, Divine* and *Ma*, along with some new tracks recorded specifically for the Playbook.

What You Need:

1. Before you start your Playbook, type bit.ly/playbooksoundtrack into your smartphone, tablet or computer browser. This is where you can listen to and download the 19 audio tracks.

2. Get a pack of crayons, colored pencils or markers and a pen for coloring and journaling!

We may each be unique in our approach to this playbook. Some of us are generally more tactile, others primarily visual while some dance to mantra and sound. In celebration of our uniqueness, below are a few suggestions:

- You can listen to each track from your device or computer and chant along.
- You can chant along and then read the pages, answering questions and taking meditations both designed to move and self inquire.
- You can chant along while coloring in the various black and white images.
- You can open into the chapter, answer the questions, and maybe have your own verbal download. Then when your moment is empty and full, you can listen and chant along to the audio recording.

At the beginning of each chapter, you will read a brief description of the specific chant that is to be expressed. These chants are mantras that have been universally sung and meditated on by spiritual seekers for centuries. A mantra is a repeated word or a phrase that holds a sacred vibration.

You will find these chants are written in Sanskrit, one of the oldest languages born from the mystical East as a means to express the language of God or Truth. We each have our own form and name for that which we connect to on a higher plane. It is said that by chanting these Sanskrit mantras, the primordial vibrations inherent can direct us to that personal calling where love and peace eternally reside, side by side.

For those who enjoy following the lyrics to the chants, they are included at the end of each chapter.

There are so many ways to explore, enter in, nurture, experiment, fall and grow!

It is my and Julie's intention that this seed serves to nurture all that you are, ever have been, always will be... and that you are more inspired to infuse our shared world with your flowering fertile essence and brilliance!

Birth away! Together! Let's Play!

Love Always,
Yvette

Table of Contents

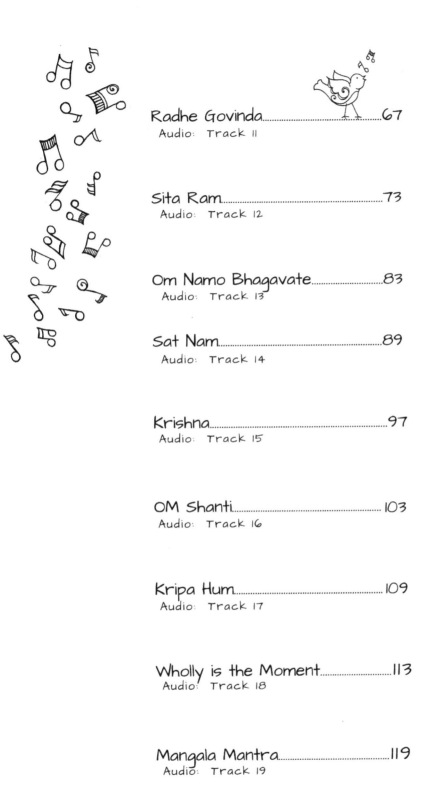

To stream & download your Playbook Soundtrack, go to: bit.ly/playbooksoundtrack
Questions? Email Yvette@YvetteOm.Com

Om

The primordial
first
sound.

Om...Try it...

Ah... the back of the throat,
Oh... the middle of the mouth.
Mmmm... the front of the lips.
Tingly there sometimes!
Amen. Ommmm. So similar.

OM emphasizes ... initializes ... transcribes
that visceral transcendant unversal
hummmmmmmmm.

We make a sound OM.

Low in the belly or
up in the chest
or even higher at our forehead.
They heard this sound in the universe: Om, AMEN ...
it was everywhere, and in all things.
A vibration in the elements of
earth, water, fire, air, and ether
The primordial first sound
from which
all other sounds are born...

Sound it whenever you need it.
OM

We are made from
sacred sound.

write it here

Sounding a big Om feels like...

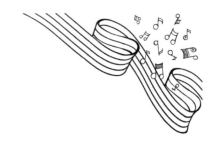

Ganesha

What is possible?

Ganesha energy is
keen, wise, self-knowing.
The more intent the focus,
the stronger your step!

ANYTHING is POSSIBLE
EVERYTHING is POSSIBLE

When we chant Ganesha, the elephant headed one, it BRINGS the energy of CLARITY.

HEAR from your SOUL

WHAT is possible?

what is the DREAM?

CLEAR away Distraction

thump
thump

thump thump

Thoughts
come and go &
can spin us like a DIZZY wind.

Chanting Ganesha energy is grounding.

Its SOLID foundation
UPROOTS interference
and POINTS us
towards the waiting soul.

Starting from a more centered
place,
we become AWARE
of a cadent, inner pulse.
It perpetuates.
We begin to MOVE with it.

can you
feel your feet?

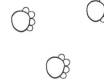

like a heartbeat

7

As we CONTINUE to focus the
energy INWARD,
the soul SINGS here I am!

Sharanam   Sharanam

Jai Ganesha!

LISTEN!
Can you hear the rythmn?
What is filling yoursoul?
you may not know!
Can you trust it?

Ganesha
energy
is

keen
wise,
self knowing.

What do you
think?

Have you
noticed?

thump
thump

can you
feel your feet?

thump
thump

The more
intent
the focus,
the stronger
your
step!

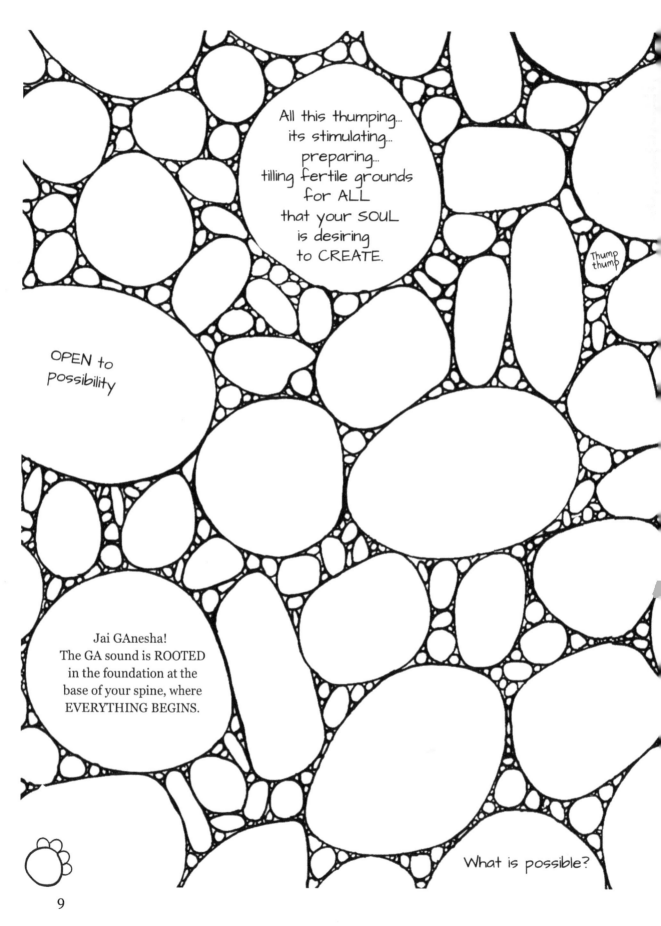

All this thumping...
its stimulating...
preparing...
tilling fertile grounds
for ALL
that your SOUL
is desiring
to CREATE.

Thump thump

OPEN to Possibility

Jai GAnesha!
The GA sound is ROOTED
in the foundation at the
base of your spine, where
EVERYTHING BEGINS.

What is possible?

9

thump
thump

Think of... the appearance of an elephant...
large in size! When we say
there is an elephant in the room,
it means there is something BIG
that we aren't acknowledging.

Thump
thump

Can you feel how
LARGE
your soul is?

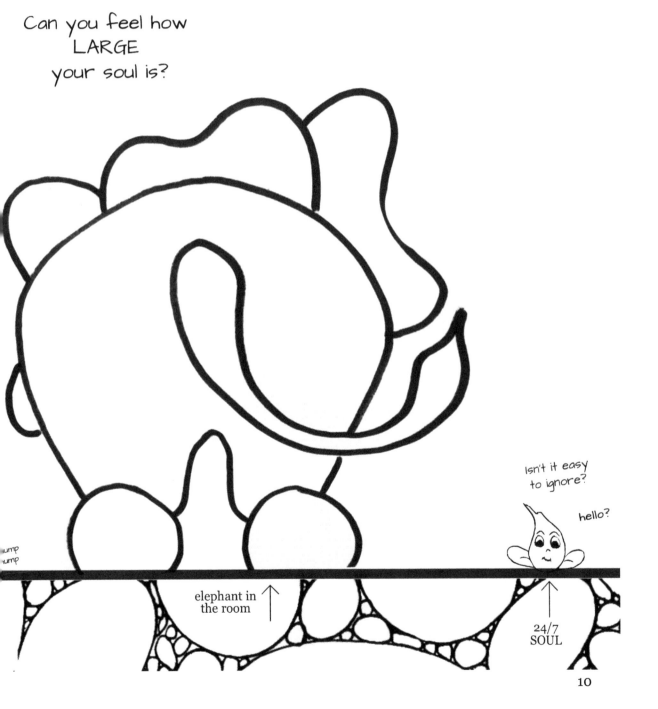

Isn't it easy
to ignore?

hello?

ump
ump

elephant in
the room ↑

24/7
SOUL ↑

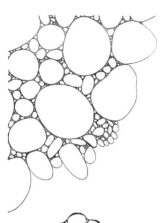

What BLOCKS you?

Write it down & take a look!

 I don't have...

 I'm afraid of....

The mind meets deterrants along the way...
can you still see the possibility?
Even then
can you MOVE FORWARD?

 I need...

 I can't...

 What will they think?

Writing STILLS the mind

What is your PULSE saying?

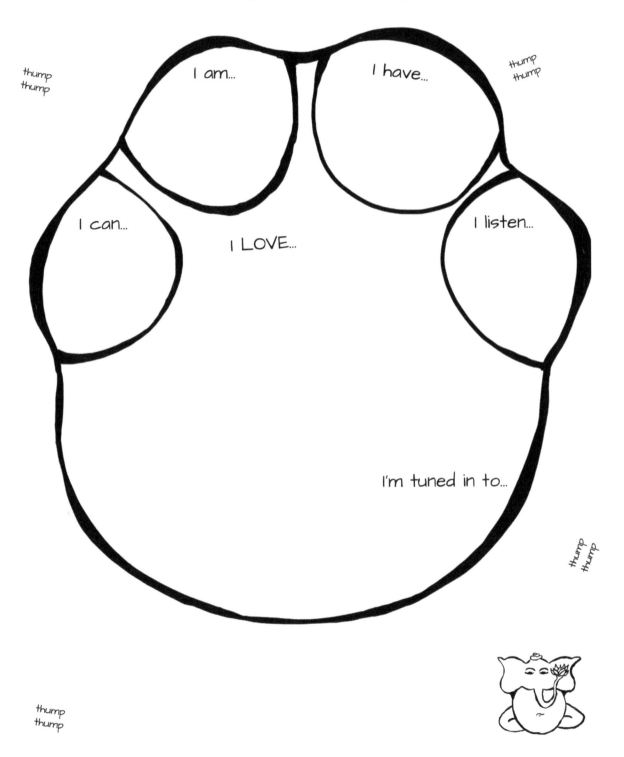

thump
thump

I am...

I have...

thump
thump

I can...

I LOVE...

I listen...

I'm tuned in to...

thump
thump

thump
thump

FEEL your pulse...
inhale, exhale...
allow breath
to let EVERYTHIING go.
Magnify purposeful pulsing
inside you & feel
the direct SYNCHRONIIZATION
of your SOUL.

What is Possible?

Jai Ganesha!

Om Ganesha Sharanam
Om Ganesha Sharanam

Om Ganesha Om
Om Ganesha Sharanam

Anything is possible

Everything is possible

Ganesha Sharanam
Ganesha Sharanam
Om Ganesha Sharanam

Sharanam Sharanam
Om Ganesha Sharanam

write it here

This is possible...

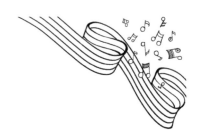

Ma

It's ALL Ma!
Affirm your birthright &
connection to the Divine.

NO THING happens without Divine Intention/Attention.

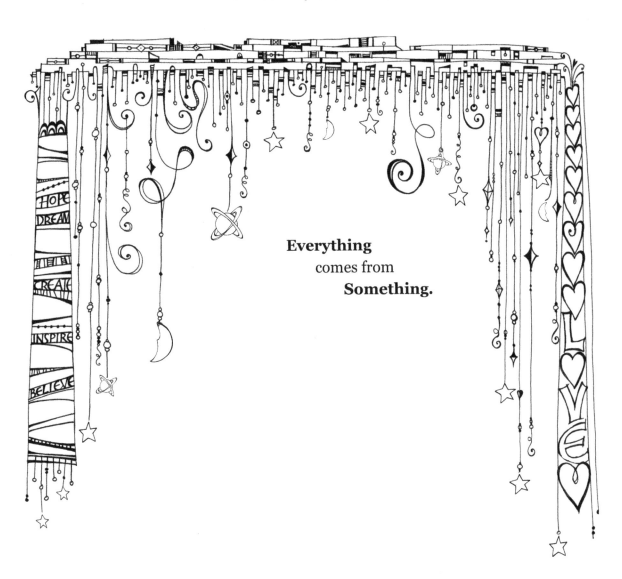

Everything
comes from
Something.

THIS is MA...

Hey
Ma!

Hey
Ma!

BIRTHING new BEGINNINGS

Each moment, each breath is a new beginning.
It's All MA!
It's MA that births us...it's Ma that cradles LIFE
in her open arms and WHISPERS to our hearts.
Listen!
It is MA who shares our deep desires,
our open and broken places.

MA
is
descending
GRACE.

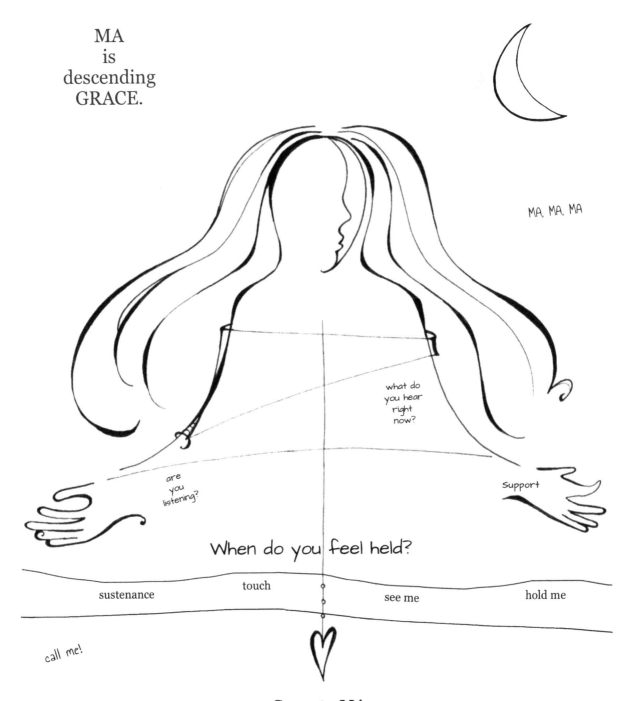

MA, MA, MA

what do
you hear
right
now?

are
you
listening?

Support

When do you feel held?

sustenance   touch   see me   hold me

call me!

Come to MA
ASK. Even when you FEAR you are not capable...
it arises in us all... doubts can cloud...
Come to MA
Affirm your birthright, and connection to the Divine.

What do you need
to GROW & THRIVE
in this Universe?

MA
has birthed YOU here...
It takes FOCUS & DESIRE
to BIRTH.
YOUR birth was INTENTIONAL.
You are here,
As you are.

There are so many names and ways to describe Ma!
Here are a few:

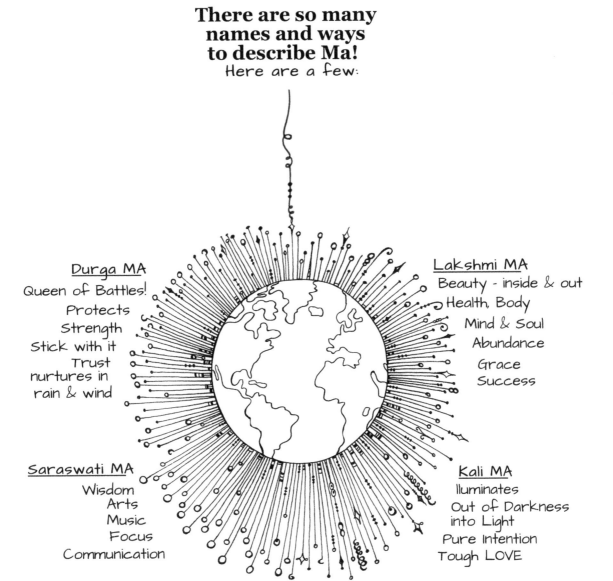

Durga MA
Queen of Battles!
Protects
Strength
Stick with it
Trust
nurtures in
rain & wind

Lakshmi MA
Beauty - inside & out
Health, Body
Mind & Soul
Abundance
Grace
Success

Saraswati MA
Wisdom
Arts
Music
Focus
Communication

Kali MA
Iluminates
Out of Darkness
into Light
Pure Intention
Tough LOVE

Do you have a name for MA?

What is she like?

How does MA show up?

songs?   people?   jokes?   animals?

What messages does MA have for you?

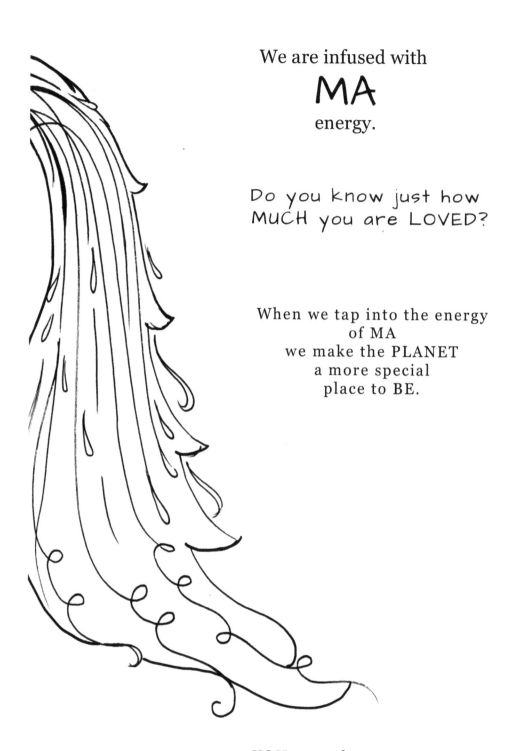

We are infused with

MA

energy.

Do you know just how
MUCH you are LOVED?

When we tap into the energy
of MA
we make the PLANET
a more special
place to BE.

YOU can always,
All ways,
SING to the energies that birthed BEAUTIFUL you.

Ma Chant Lyrics

Birthing new beginnings
Hey Ma, Hey Ma

Ma Durga
Hey Ma

Kali Ma
Hey Kali Ma

Jai Ma Ma Ma

Lakshmi Ma
Hey Ma

Saraswati Ma

Jai Ma Ma Ma

Mata Kali Ma
Mata Durge Ma
Mata Lakshmi Ma
Saraswati Ma
Mata Ambe Ma
Parashakti Ma

Om Ma

write it here

What is birthing in my life?

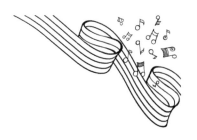

Gate

Whatever we perceive to be lost...
is actually in the
process
of transformation.

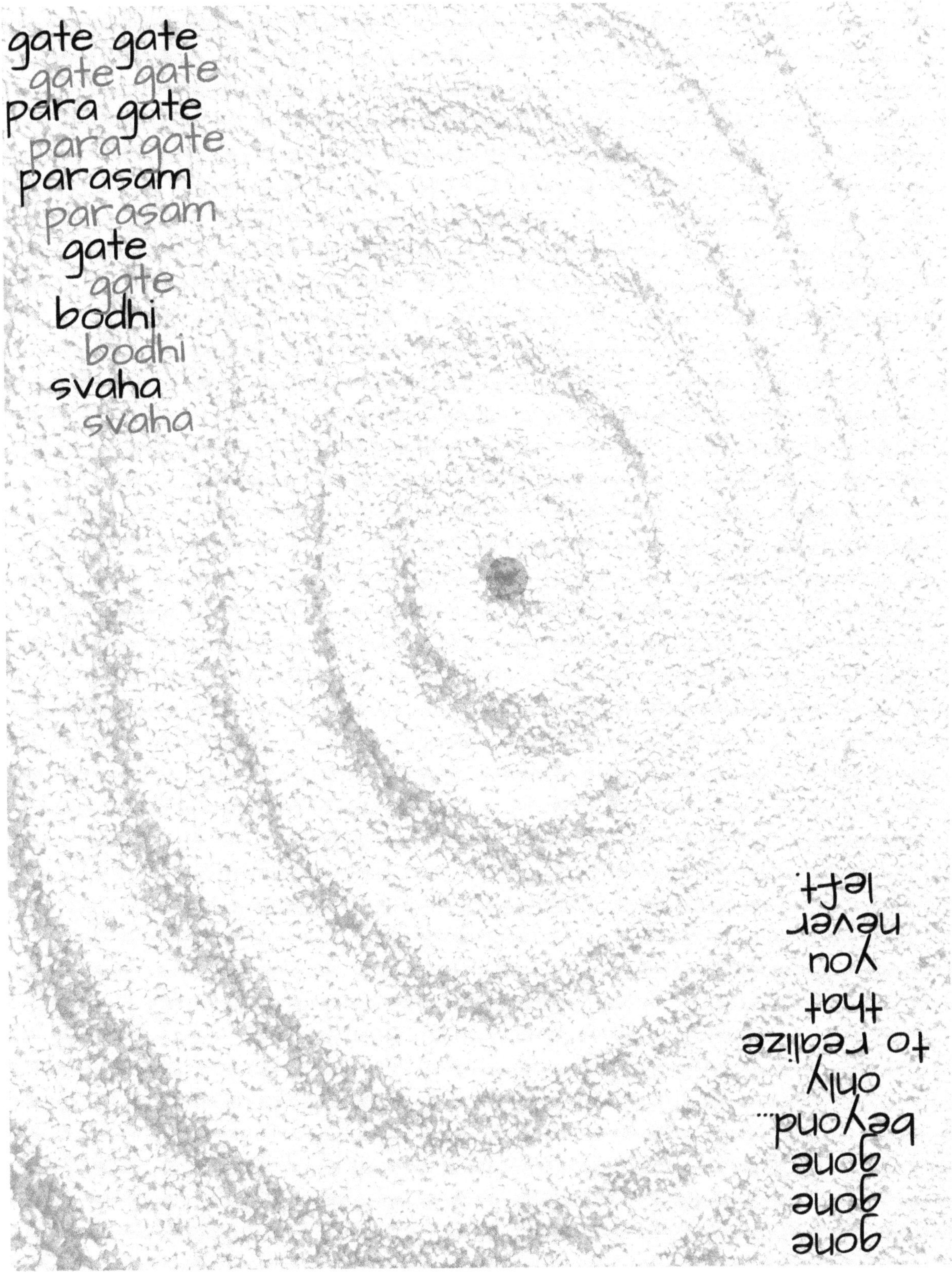

gate gate
gate gate
para gate
para gate
parasam
parasam
gate
gate
bodhi
bodhi
svaha
svaha

gone
gone
gone
beyond...
only
to realize
that
you
never
left

Do we ever really LOSE anything?
Or does it just CHANGE... to BECOME something else?
(Well, it has to, or things would ALWAYS be the same.)
Just because we can't see it with our EYES
doesn't mean it isn't there.

What have you lost lately?

How did your life change?

Did you change too?

gate   gate   para gate   parasam

gate   bodhi   svaha

When we lose something, is it ever really gone?
I mean the ESSENCE, the FEELING of it?
Does it still hold meaning for you?
Maybe EVEN MORE meaning because it left?

ne, gone, gone beyond...

gate   gate   para   gate   parasam   gate   bodhi   svaha

CHANGE TRANSFORMS.

Gone, gone, gone beyond
...only to realize that you never left

This is the Buddah's
realization before his passing.
How many things in this
universe are happening
without our seeing it?

HOLD the gift of the Buddha
in
the
JEWEL
of your
Heart

Whatever
we
perceive
to be
lost is actually
in the
process
of transformation.

Behind the CHANGE rests
the CHANGE-LESS.

What do you tend to
cling to?

What about...
clinging to the changeless?

IF you have to
cling at all.

REST within the
CHANGELESS.
TRUST that the moving
images...
the comings...
the goings...
that make up the STORY of
your LIFE...
have no ENDING and no
BEGINNING.

Heart Sutra Lyrics

Gate
Gate
Paragate
Parasam Gate
Bodhi Svaha

Gone
Gone
Attain the other shore having never left

write it here

I can more fully embrace the gift of change by...

Take Down the Sound

Chanting Radhe
attracts a vibration
called Shakti...
the active part of love.

HEAR what's
in my
SOUL

TAKE IT DOWN

expand
contract
BeLow Sound
expand

Turn down the noise

TAKE IT DOWN

a watchful warrior is not afraid

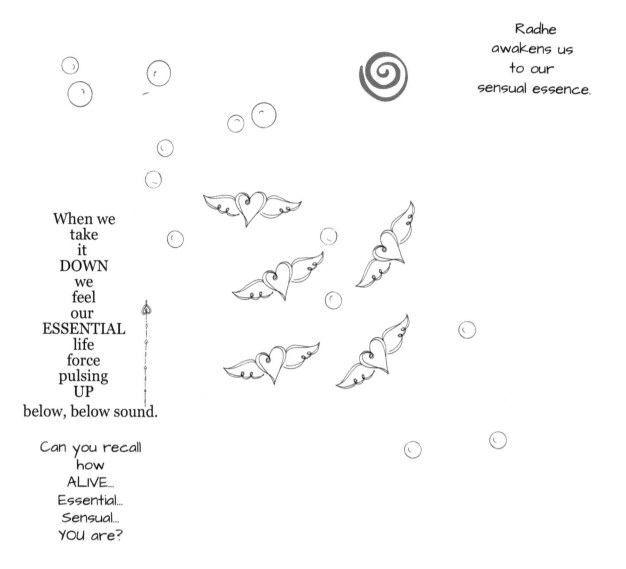

Radhe
awakens us
to our
sensual essence.

When we
take
it
DOWN
we
feel
our
ESSENTIAL
life
force
pulsing
UP
below, below sound.

Can you recall
how
ALIVE...
Essential...
Sensual...
YOU are?

LIFE manifests everything within
its limitless space.....all form of
matter. From the dense boulder to
the teeny bed bug.
When we break it down ᵉwww!
there are only floating atoms.

SHED those excuses...and all the outer layers...
empty out...empty in
How does it feel?

scary?

liberating?
both?

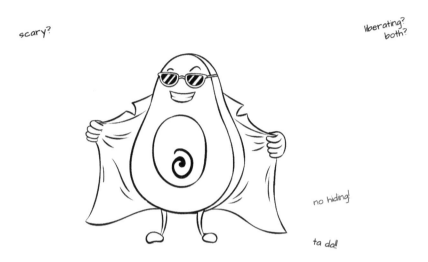

no hiding!

ta da!!

EXPOSE your sensually AWAKE self.

It's an active PRACTICE of
INNER engagement...
NOT a numbing...
covering up...
checking out...

It is
CONNECTING &
RECONNECTING
to a SPACE that is PALPABLE.

Can YOU take it DOWN?

active.....alive......open.....expand.....contract.....empty out

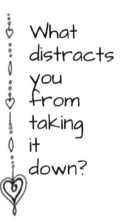

What
distracts
you
from
taking
it
down?

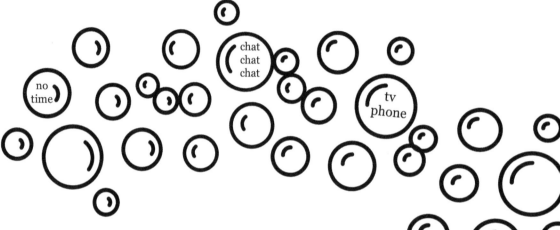

chat
chat
chat

no time

tv phone

Noise, technology, time, movement turn our attention towards temporary highs, those distracting and quickly satisfying rides.
The danger of being overly immersed with the commute is that once the ride is over, things can seem quite a downer. It is harder to land in the heart & find our inner compass.

We land so far from the pure, free Self. Back on the ground we find ourself directionless.

It's harder to get in to self... where it really lives.
Do you look to the outside world to feel the sensual?

ROLLER COASTER

Off the strain

Turn OFF the VOLUME

Loosen the heartstrings

Free up the juice

Take
a BIG
Breath
Take it in
s l o w
hold it
then
LET IT ALL GO

pop
pop

When you get this close....
    what is left?

Close your eyes...
can you feel
where your skin
ends?

It's
all
in
nothing

naked self

and nothing in all

Take Down the Sound Lyrics. Radhe Radhe!

Take down the sound
Turn off the volume
Let me hear what is in my soul
Turn down the noise
Loosen the heartstrings
Look in for that empty void

Radhe Radhe

Free up the juice
Jack up the focus
Bare the truth the naked self
Ease off the strain
Building awareness
For a watchful warrior is not afraid

Radhe Radhe

It's all in no-thing and no-thing is all

Tune into frequency
The slick vibration
Silence as the witness leads the way
Turn down the noise
Turn up the volume
Subtle consciousness is here to stay

Radhe Radhe

 When I get really quiet inside, I experience...

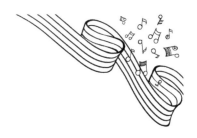

Samadhi

Samadhi
is being one
with ONE.

It is PEACE, Samadhi
Being ONE with ONE
just Peace, Samadhi
Bliss... Bliss

It is PEACE, Samadhi
no pain, No joy
just Peace, Samadhi
the iNNER voice

It is PEACE, Samadhi
lighten up the outer glow
just peace, Samadhi
as the fire inside you grows

Dive Deep... Breath Low

write it here

My inner voice is saying...

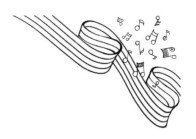

Shiva

This is the formless energy
that walks within.

SHIVA energy is formless, intelligence, consciousness...
the backdrop behind which everything happens.
As life itself is in a state of perpetual change,
this transformational energy breaks down
whatever needs to be destroyed
in order for it to be reborn & reformed.

DISRUPTION!
It can be so **messy**.
Sometimes it's hard to LET GO
when we feel we are not ready to
or when we DON'T KNOW what's coming next.

How do YOU deal with DISRUPTION when it suddenly shows up?

Check all that apply:

___ dread

___ excitement

___ head in the sand

___ inquisitive

___ resistance

___ bring it on

___ victim

___ leap of faith

___ confusion

___ insomnia

___ nervous giggles

___ stress eating

___ this:_____

___ all of the above

Ultimately
TRANSFORMATIONAL energy
imprints
a spiritual & peaceful gait.

Can you
synchronize your STEPS
with this transcendent energy?

What can your imprint be?

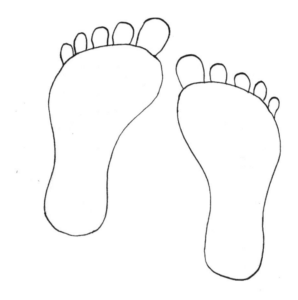

TRY this walking meditation. Consider each
step as if it were a PRAYER.

As you chant
Om Na-Mah Shiva-Ya,
acknowledge your
transcendence
one syllable,
one step at a time.

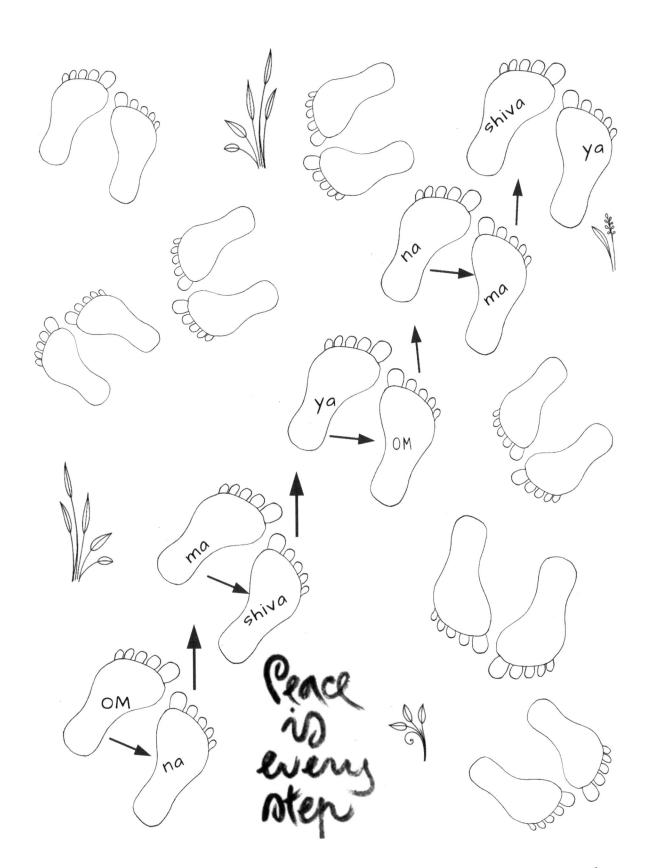

Panchakshara Lyrics
(5 syllable mantra)

Namah Shivaya

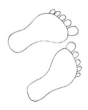

 write
it here

Each step is intentional movement towards...

Hanuman

It's about selflessness.
Less self
to lift humanity
up on its wings.

**HANUMAN
CHALISA**

**It's about
Seva.**

**Selflessness
less self
more heart
remembering
forgetting**

We SING to
remember our
place in the world.

40 verses!
So long!
In sanskrit!
What's it all mean?

Hanuman
forgot
all the time!

The Chalisa chants to that part of ourself that
KNOWS it can do anything when it comes to helping others.
We become super-human beings!
We have the power inside to touch others,
say that exact right thing
to lift humanity up on it's wings.

It's
a
meditation
with a
monkey!

It's a STREAM of consciousness...
There are some who say that just before we pass, WE SEE a projection of
all the MOMENTS in our lives
that MATTERED most.
Maybe its the SMALL and the effortless things we did.
When we SMILED to a stranger...
SAT with an Elder...
Brought brownies to a friend when they were DOWN
or SOUP when they were SICK...
offered an out of the way RIDE...
CUDDLED a crying baby...
We FILL UP the SOUL
when we are IN service...
no reaching for recognition, reward, credit.

Look inward and back,
drawing from memory...
name the moments that will matter the most

so
many!

Who are my real life super heros?

Hanuman Chalisa Lyrics

The Hanuman Chalisa is one of the most chanted prayers written in the ancient language of Sanskrit. It is said that when this 40 verse Chalisa is chanted, Hanuman can remember his true power. With every chanted verse perhaps we, like Hanuman, can awaken the sacred potency of our own gifts. Let's gracefully recall the superhuman divinity breathing within us all.

Invocation

Shri Guru Charana Sarooja-raja, Nija manu Mukura Sudhaari

Baranau Rahubhara Bimala Jaso, Jo Dayaku Pala Chari

Budhee-Heena Tanu Jannikay, Sumirow Pavana Kumara

Bala-Budhee Vidya Dehoo Mohee, Harahu Kalesha Vikaara

Chalisa Verses

Jai Hanumana gyana gun sagar, Jaya Kapisha tihun lok ujagar

Ram doot atulit bal dhama, Anjaani-putra Pavana suta nama

Mahabira Bikrama Bajrangi, Kumati nivara sumati Ke sangi

Kanchana varana viraja subesa, Kanana Kundalaa Kunchta Kesha

Hatha Vajra Aura Dhuvaje Viraje, Kaandhe moonja janehu sajai

Shankara suvana kesri Nandan, Teja prataapa maha jaga bandan

Bidyavaana guni ati chatur, Rama kaja karibe ko aatur

Prabu charitra sunibe-ko rasiya, Rama Lakhana Sita mana Basiya

Sukshma roopa dhari Siyahin dikhava, Bikata roopa dhari lanka jarava

Bhima roopa dhari asura sanghare, Ramachandra ke kaja sanvare

Laye Sanjivana Lakhana Jiyaye, Shri Raghuvira Harashi ur laye

Raghupati Kinhi bahuta barai, Tuma mama priye Bharata-hi-sama bhai

Sahasa badana tumharo jasha gaave, Asa-kahi Shripati kanta lagaave

Sanakadhika Brahmaadi Muneesa, Narada-Sharad sahita Aheesa

Yam Kubera Digpaala Jahan te, Kabi kobid kahi sake kahan te

Tum upkara Sugreevahin keenha, Rama milaye rajpada deenha

Tumharo mantra bibheeshana maana, Lankeshwara Bhaye Saba jaga jana

Yug sahastra jojana para Bhanu, Leelyo tahi madhura phal janu

Prabhu mudrika meli mukha maheen, Jaladhi langhi gaye achraja naheen

Durgaama kaja jagatha ke jete, Sugama anugraha tumhre tete

Rama dwaare tuma rakhvar, Hoata na agya binu paisare

Saba sukha lahae tumhari shara na, Tuma rakshaka kahu ko dara naa

Aapana teja samharo aapai, Teenhon loka hanka ten kanpai

Bhoota pisaacha Nikata nahin aavai, Mahabira jaba naama sunavae

Nase roga harae saba peera, Japata nirantara Hanumata beera

Sankat te Hanuman churavae, Mana Karama Bachana dyana jo lavai

Saba para Rama tapasvee raja, Tina ke kaja sakala Tuma saja

Aura manoratha jo koi lavai, Sohi amita jeevana pala pavai

Charon Juga paratapa tumhara, Hai persidha jagata ujiyara

Sadhu Santa ke tuma Rakhware, Asura nikandana Rama dulhare

Ashta-sidhi nau nidhi ke dhata, As-bara deena Janki mata

Rama rasayana tumhare pasa, Sada raho Raghupati ke das

Tumhare bhajana Rama ko pavai, Janama-janama ke dukh bisraavai

Antha-kaala Raghubara pur jayee, Jahan janama Hari-Bakhta Kahaye

Aur Devta Chita na dharehi, Hanumata se hi sarve sukha karehi

Sankata kate-mite saba peera, Jo sumirai Hanumata Balbeera

Jai Jai Jai Hanumana Gosahin, Kripa Karahu Gurudeva ki nyahin

Jo sata bara patha kare kohi, Chutehi bandhi maha sukh hohi

Jo yaha parhe Hanumana Chalisa, Hoye siddhi sakhi Gaureesa

Tulsidasa sada hari chera, Keejai Natha Hridaye mahan dera

Pavana Tanaya Sankata Harana, Mangala Murati Roopa

Rama Lakhana Sita Sahita, Hridaya Basahu Soora Bhoo

I serve the world when I...

Radhe Govinda

Sing to the energies
that sing
in the name of love!

This is a story of a young mother
on a VERY dark & stormy day...

A hurricane struck...
and randomly blew
so many houses DOWN...

While the alarms were sounding
she returned,
only to find her beautiful HOME
had FALLEN to the ground...

Despite her traumatic loss
she RACED around her town...
checking on neighbors
to make sure they
and their families were
SAFE and SOUND...

FILLING water buckets and
carrying them
from here to there,
by morning
she had
completely FORGOTTEN
her own despair...

Hooray
for
LOVE!

No matter how
high the tide,
a new dawn will
bring peaceful
skies.

Radhe
Govinda
Radhe Gopal

Our way
will
ALWAYS
be,
Always
Love.

Hari
Bol!

SING! SING for LOVE!

No matter how hard
we fall...
the mountains are
standing up tall...

Can you recall a
RISING UP to the
call of LOVE...
When you forgot
yourself in that
compassion and ran
to the aid of
another?

What did it feel like?

No matter how lonely we feel

69

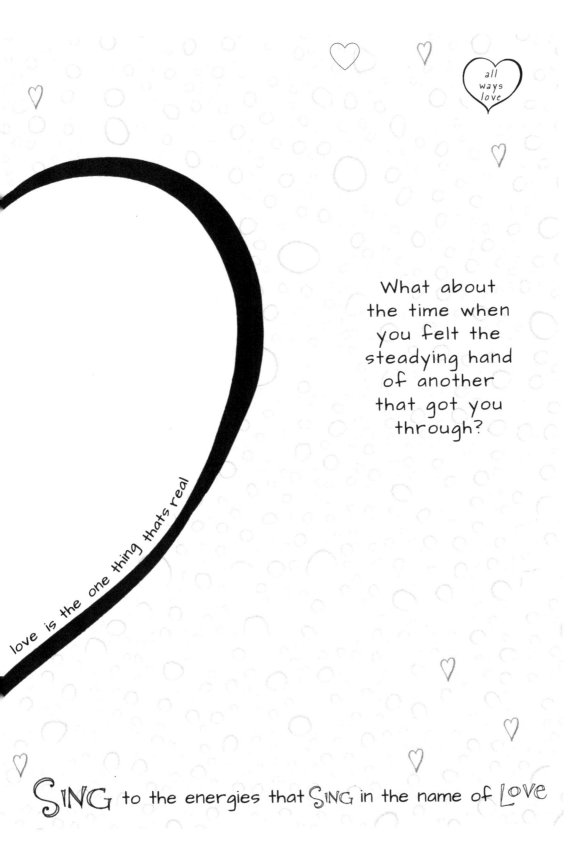

all
ways
love

What about
the time when
you felt the
steadying hand
of another
that got you
through?

love is the one thing thats real

SING to the energies that SING in the name of LOVE

Always Love

In the throws of Mother Nature
Come changes in the dark
And the orison beseeching brings the gaze back to the light
We are born into illusion
And the truth is hard to see
On the other side of shadow is the love we all can be

No matter how it goes
However the winds they blow
Our way will always be
Always Love

No matter how hard we fall
The mountains are standing up tall
And our way will always be
Always Love

Radhe Govinda Radhe Gopal

Radha Hare Radha Hare

Jai Jai Govinda Jai Haribol

Haribol Haribol Haribol

No matter how high the tide
A new dawn will bring peaceful skies
And our way will always be
Always Love

No matter when shadow comes
Our children can look to the suns
And our way will always be
Always Love

write it here

Love is calling me to...

Hari Bol!

Sita Ram

**The dance
of opposites.**

Merge... I want to merge Heaven & Earth.

Where are you right now?

Do you feel good?

How do you relate to nature?

Do you feel lighthearted when you are strolling
on the beach or hiking down a mountain?

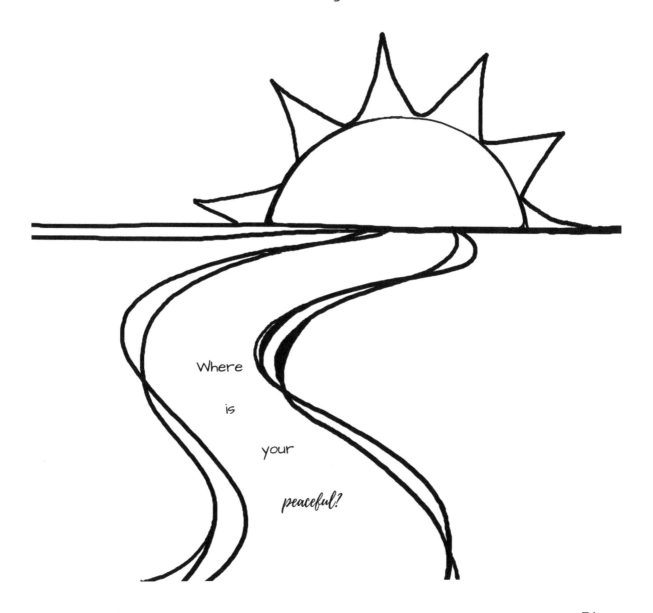

Where

is

your

peaceful?

Is it POSSIBLE that nature outside is MIRRORING
the part of you inside that is also beautiful & peaceful?

Can you spend more time with those parts of YOURSELF that you really LOVE? ?

The MIRROR works BOTH ways

Sri Ram   Jai Ram   Jai Jai Ram

DEEP
in the abyss
of
BLISS

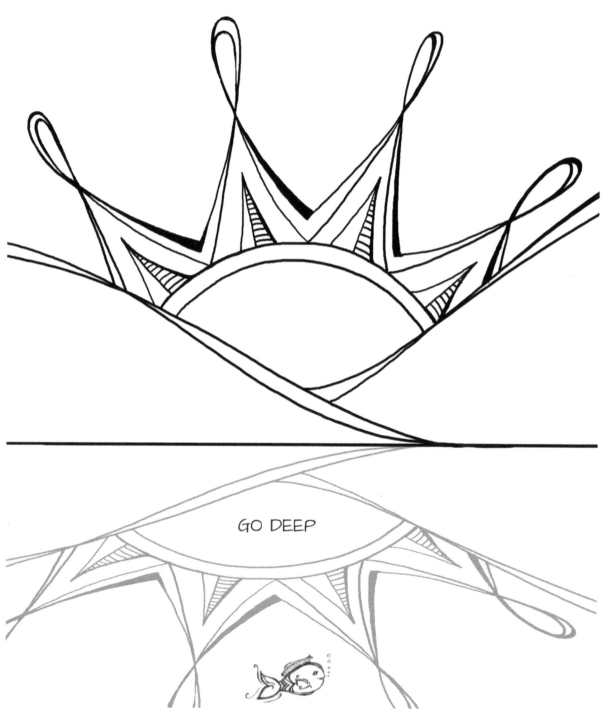

GO DEEP

MERGE

seen & unseen

heaven & earth

good times bad times

Sita Ram
Sita Ram

old & new

When it all

breaks down

isn't it
all the same?

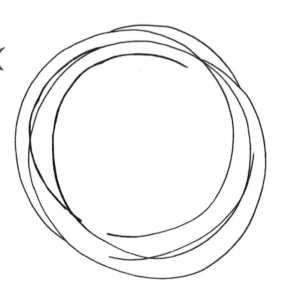

here there

I am you
you are me
this is the true heaven we seek.

Sita

Ram

Sita Moon:
feminine
reflective
flowy
emotion
intution
receptive

What
does
the
moon
tell you
on a
dark,
starry
night?

Rama Sun:
hot
masculine
aggressive
radiant
courageous
energizing
outgoing

What
does
the
sun
share
with
you on
a
bright
day?

Do you
see these
within you?

They are both there!

Do you lean
more towards
one or
the other?

We are all made
in a
special way.

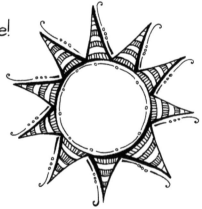

WATCH the Divine Play.

Merge

Embracing ALL
aspects of life...
all her color...
variation...
polarity...
form.

Can you hold it all?

masculine or *feminine,*
or
a little of both.

Can you *dance* with these
opposite forces at *play?*

Merge Heaven & Earth Lyrics

I want to merge
with the bird and the sun
and the heart
merge into the soul of pure light

I want to merge
with the stone and the moon
and the dove
merge into the womb of pure love

Deep in the abyss of bliss
I want to merge heaven and earth

I am you ~ you are me ~
this is the true heaven we seek

Sri Ram Jai Ram Jai Jai Ram
Sri Ram Jai Ram Jai Jai Ram

Sita Ram

 write it here

I embrace all the colors of myself by....

Om Namo Bhagavate

Receive
the nectar of remembering....
I am Divine!

OM NAMO

SINGING
to your soul.

BHAGAVATE

The personal and separate soul
keeps forgetting its infinite nature...
like a piece of itself,
or someone/something
is missing... longing.

VASUDEVAYA

The infinite soul
(never forgets its true nature.)

I am divine!

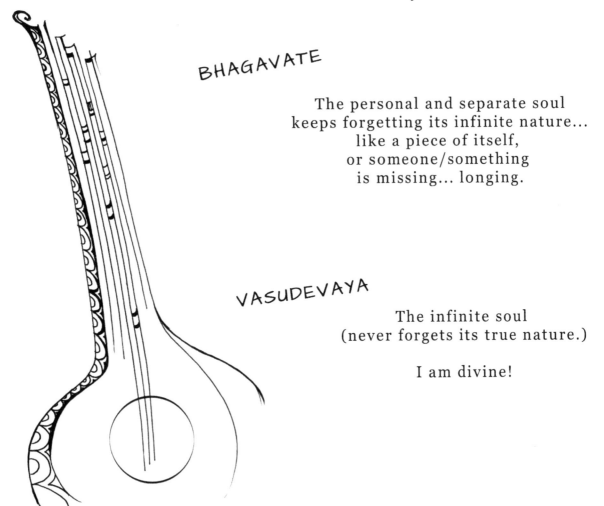

OM NAMO BHAGAVATE
VASUDEVAYA

Its like riding a bike!

I forgot!

again!

Put them together...
I forget...
I remember...

remember...
forget...
remember...
forget...
whoops!

This is the divine dance...
we get the
**SWEETNESS of
remembering,**
EVERY time!

Receive the nectar
of remembering...
I AM divine!

On & on it goes....

HRIT Padma
The flame of the soul,
just below the heart.
It's ALWAYS there.

Om Namo Bhagavate Lyrics

Om Namo
Bhagavate
Vasudevaya

Om Namo
Namo Namo
Hari Om

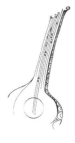

I am divinely inspired...

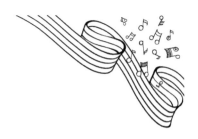

Sat Nam

I
AM.

SAT NAM

**While letting go
we will KNOW
how to just BE**

Still...

silent...

listening...

shhhhhh

What do you hear?

What are you feeling?

What are you thinking?

Is it you? What is true?

What roles do you play?

so many!

How many hats do you wear?

So many different kinds out there!

Can you be more here in this space?

calm... quiet... listening...
so still you can hear the inner voice.
I am, it says, I am.

I am what?

Well, we wear all those hats...
mother, brother, friend, baker,
hat maker, purple haired rocker...
all roles have a hat to wear.

But WHO is really there?

sat nam

That part that NEVER changes
speaks
I AM
Sat Nam.
It's the one thing
thats real.

So much of the time
we come, we go,
and within all that
we can HEAR
I AM...I AM
that NEVER changes.

Take OFF your hats
and STAY awhile...
SIT in your SPACE...
it is GRACE

let go!

See what is true

See what is true

See what is true

IN YOU

Sat Nam Lyrics

Sit in the grace of your space and be
Shine in the glow of your light and be

I Am Sat Nam

Follow the love in your soul and be
While letting go we will know how to just be

I Am Sat Nam

Sit in your place of truth and be
Like water bathing in the seas - just be

Be in your space of truth - it is you
The goddess seeking what is true - it is you

I Am Sat Nam

See what is true in you

write it here

I am...

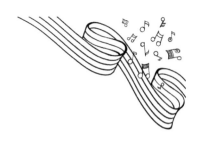

Krishna

The energy of Krishna ignites
the *infinite,*
magic,
mystery of
movement.

PLAY all day
with the divine
unseen...
DROP it all and RUN
out into the open field
feeling absolutely SEEN... ADORED...
just as you are?

What if
you would...

Come out
and play!

The energy of Krishna is followed
like the Pied Piper.
When we feel that spark of inner delight,
we connect with the
infinite
magic
mystery
of movement.
It spontaneously FLOWS.

Are
you
serious?

I've been
waiting
for you
to play!

BREATHE into your empty,
waiting vessel...
like a flute yet to be played
as never before.

What kind of PLAY is wanting
to express through you?

walking
barefoot

swimming

spinning
around

dancing
solo

skinny
dipping

finger
painting

belly
laughing

singing big

howling at
the moon

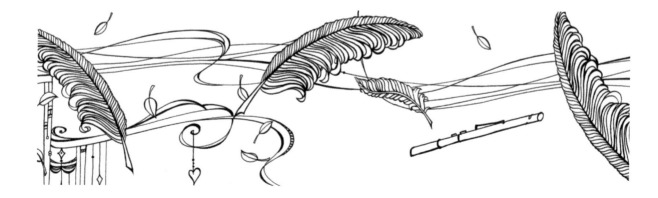

Hey Bhagavan...
The Maha Mantra is a
TIMELESS song
that has been sung
for ages & ages.
Vasudevo...
Boundless, Infinite...
Always has, is & will be

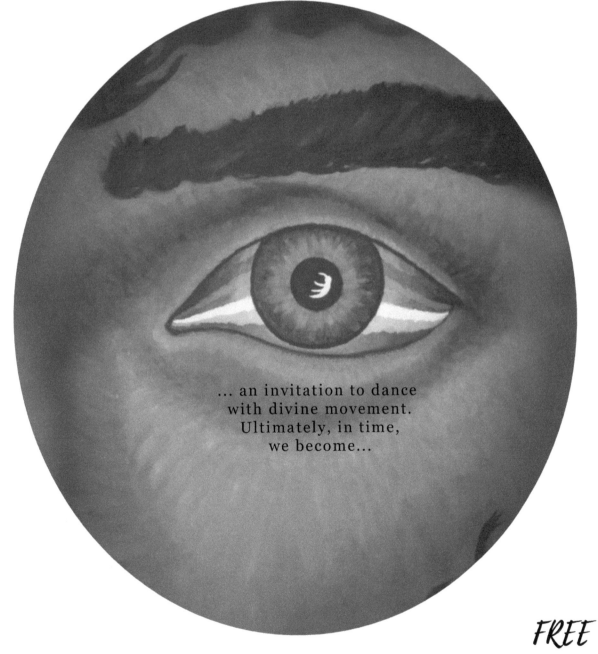

... an invitation to dance
with divine movement.
Ultimately, in time,
we become...

FREE

Krishna Lyrics
the Maha Mantra

Hare Krishna
Hare Krishna
Krishna Krishna
Hare Hare

Hare Rama
Hare Rama
Rama Rama
Hare Hare

Sri Krishna, Damodara,
Hey Bhagavan
Vasudevo

Sri Krishna,
Govinda Hari
Vasudevo

write it here

I open to the magic mystery of me...

Om Shanti

The sound of Peace
is Universal.

WE ARE ONE
in this world.
If I give my heart to you...
will you always be there?

peace

salām

shalom

śānti

śānti

shalom

We are all children... vulnerable. When we share our gifts, ourselves, we are as exposed as a defenseless child; sometimes, we feel we need to cover it up, or hold back.

Can we know & treat each other
with this awareness?

We are different people,
yet we are ONE in this truth.
We breathe together...
we share the same fears, desires.

Can we be more familiar to oneness than differences?

I am you, you are me;
THIS is the true heaven we seek.

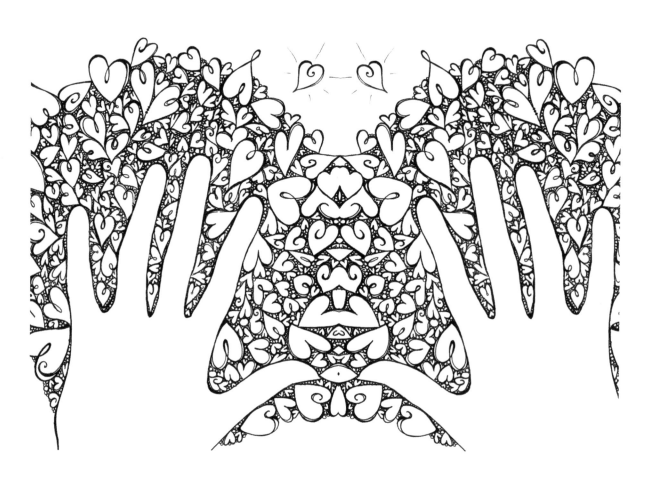

We are One Lyrics

If I give my heart to you
Will you always be there
For I'm frightned of the things I don't know
And if I share my light with you
Will you promise to be true
For I'm longing to know all of you

We are one in this world
We are one
And we are one in this life
We are one

At the sun's rise we are one
In a child's eyes we are one
In the emptiness of darkness we are one

We are one in this world
We are one
And when it's all said and done
We are one

Om shanti Om
shanti, shanti

Hallelujah

Shalom Aleichem

Assalamu Alaikum

We are one in this world

write it here

My vision of peace is...

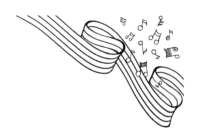

Kripa Hum

Divine Bliss.
I am that.

Divine grace.
This is ALL Divine grace...
by the grace of...
Amazing Grace.

Consider the possibility that
you are
Divine grace.

What opens within you?

Can you EMBRACE
Joy? Bliss? Ease? Freedom?

Kripa Hum.
Divine Grace.

So Hum.
This is so.

Ananda Hum.
I am Bliss.

Let's Celebrate!

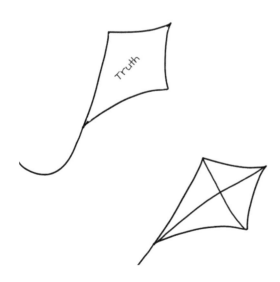

Kripa Hum Lyrics

Kripa Hum

Ananda Hum

Truth Bliss Consciousness

write it here

Bliss expresses through me as...

Wholly is the Moment

Each moment...
If you treat it with reverence, you notice the
miracle.

Nothing
happens
without
that
divine  spark
from
which
we
emanate.

Each

MOMENT

a meditation in PRESENCE.

Return to the sacred again & again.

Wholly is the

moment

when I

breathe...

hear...

beat...

feel...

speak...

when we

stand...

Wholly is the

the moment

when I

see..

Wholly

 write it here

Wholly is the moment when I...

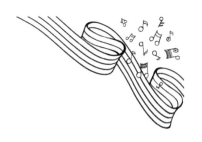

Mangala Mantra

A universal prayer to bless our
beloved world.

Lokah Samastah Sukhino Bhavantu

May ALL beings be happy & free.
May my thoughts, words and actions
contribute in some way to
that happiness and freedom for ALL.

Come, take a look. Closer. What do you see?

I am the Universe both manifest and unmanifest.
I am the Trinity.
I simultaneously create, contain and decease.
My layers of complexity... Infinite.

Can you see me in this mystical geometrical diagram
called the Sri Yantra?

People around the world have meditated
upon this image for centuries.

They still do.

It is believed that when you concentrate on these
9 interlocking triangles, making up
43 smaller, within 2 concentric circles and outer squares
it unleashes mental CLARITY,
FREEDOM from suffering... PEACE.

Can you find me at the center point,
what is called the Bindu?

Can you recognize... Can you find you?

I bless the world...

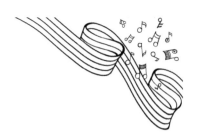

Acknowledgement

We'd like to acknowledge the ancient and timeless
wisdoms gifted to us from the East. Especially
the Universal teachings of Yoga and Mantra
channeled by Rishis and Saints, and brought to
the West by such Master teachers as
Paramahansa Yogananda, Swami Satchidananda,
Amritanandamayi and other enlightened souls.
Your loving guidance for humanity continues as a
blessing that lights our way.

To our readers and community, we thank you
for your support. It is our wish & prayer that
this Playbook serves you;
breath by breath
word by word
song by song ...
One in voice and all ways love.

About the Authors

Yvette Om is a singer, poet, songwriter, intuitive and chant artist with a passion for awakening the hidden song within us all. She has recorded many celebrated albums that marry the ancient healing chanting of Sanskrit mantra with inspiring English lyrics. Yvette is also a yoga teacher, and a meditation and mantra coach. She loves to bring people together to hold up the mystical mirror, while exploring the infinite nature of each participant through a variety of workshops, kirtan and retreats. She currently resides in Pennsylvania with her husband Christopher, her two daughters and a furry, four-pawed beloved Buddy. To learn more about Yvette or to contact her please visit www.YvetteOm.com

Julie Fischer is a student of Yvette Om, as well as a co-dreamer of projects and events with her. She is a novice but sincere mantra chanter & harmonium player, who loves to travel. She is also a yoga teacher, massage therapist, interfaith minister, mother of two fabulous women and nana of three grandchildren. juliefischerwellness.com

About the Illustrators

Joanne Fink Zenspirations® founder Joanne Fink is an award-winning designer, calligrapher, best-selling author, and spiritual seeker who loves helping people tap into their innate creative gifts. Joanne spent 20 years designing and developing products for the gift, stationery, craft, and faith-based markets and leads virtual and in-person workshops all over the world. www.zenspirations.com

Christopher A. Pecoraro has been an artist his entire life. He has performed on Broadway in musicals and is currently an artist who prefers to create with oil on canvas. He is a graduate of the Pennsylvania Academy of Fine Arts in Philadelphia and the American Academy of Dramatic Arts in New York. Christopher feels blessed to have been able to work as a painter, singer and actor. Christopherpec.com